CONTENTS

AMAZON FBA: THE COMPLETE GUIDE 2019

Bring your business from $ 0 to
$ 9000 in 30 days!

Are you interested in starting a new business on Amazon? Do you want to start an e-commerce project and quickly make it a profitable business? Or do you simply want to diversify your sales channels, proposing yourself also within the most famous and important marketplace in the world?

Whatever your needs, you're definitely in the right place! In fact we have created for you a complete guide for selling on Amazon, full of tips to be exploited and applied immediately. Ready?

E-COMMERCE OR AMAZON?

Many people wonder if it is better to sell on their website rather than on Amazon to reach their sales goals.

Well, the mistake is ... in the question! Your website and your page on Amazon are two completely different sales tools that, in addition, are not even alternative (if anything, complementary).

Amazon is like a big "mall" or, perhaps more correctly, a "department store" where every seller has his corner. The rich selection of products that users can find inside the marketplace is just one of the factors that encourage customers to return frequently on these pages.

Bestseller: Giochi e giocattoli

Not only that Amazon has a large customer base that very often look right on the site of Jeff Bezos before looking for their products elsewhere (and this happens in particular for Prime subscribers).

Therefore, your website is not an alternative way to sell on Amazon.

Suffice it to consider that in order to get traffic on your "commercial" website you will have to acquire it with specific promotional and marketing activities, and that this - as we will see - is only one of the many distinctive points that you will have to take into account in your comparison analysis between the two selling methods.

So, from these first parts of our guide, don't think of Amazon as a sort of "cannibal" towards traffic on your website, or as a unique path to pursue with an insane passion. Consider it rather as a supplementary channel to those already existing or that you will develop, and that can be used in synergy with your website, framing all sales channels within a broader marketing strategy!

ADVANTAGES AND DISADVANTAGES OF SELLING ON AMAZON

One of the reasons that should lead you to consider Amazon as a "collaborative" and non-substitute channel, is the fact that the

Bezos marketplace has the following distinctive elements.

Among the positive distinctive elements, we can certainly

remember how Amazon allows you to:

• get in touch with hundreds of millions of potential customers: if you are not present on Amazon, you are probably losing important opportunities to make your brand known and, consequently,

increase your sales;

• use a simple platform, as this is the process of selling your products on Amazon. All you will be asked to do is register on Amazon and insert your products in the catalog, then administering every detail thanks to the management panel of your merchant

account;

• use a logistics service that - as we will see - will also give you the opportunity to allow Amazon to manage 100% of your sales logistics, from the storage of goods

to shipping and return management.

As we anticipated you a few lines ago, there are certainly no negative distinctive elements or, at least, the points on

which you will necessarily have to pay attention.

Think, for example, of the risk (often, a fear not

comforted by reality) of:

• lose the "control" on your customers: customers who buy on your Amazo account are from Amazon, and not yours. This of course does not mean that you cannot, through appropriate strategies, transform them into loyal customers, but only that by selling through Amazon you will not have access to a series of

very important information to optimize your business;

• create excessive dependence on Amazon: as we have had occasion to remember several times, Amazon will not cannibalize your website or other sales channels, but an excessive exposure to it could lead you to the temptation to neglect your e-com-

merce reducing perhaps the uses in other marketing activities;

• end up in the vortex of competition: more and more companies are choosing to sell on Amazon and, if it is true that this is an important component of the marketplace's success, it is also true that you will find yourself in a very strong scenario of competi-

tion.

As you can well imagine, in reality none of the points mentioned above is necessarily a benefit or a disadvantage. Everything depends on the way in which you will be able to realize a vast marketing strategy that, within it, also includes a conscious and sus-

tainable way to be present on Amazon!

HOW MUCH DOES IT COST TO SELL ON AMAZON?

Introduced the above, we try to get more into our guide and ask how much it costs to sell on Amazon.

Even if the marketplace will allow you to access a series of excellent services with high efficiency and wide satisfaction, it is also true that if you want to make your business fully sustainable on this channel you will still have to put a dedicated budget into account.

Fortunately for you, however, this is certainly not an excessively onerous investment: let's see together how much to allocate to start selling on the Jeff Bezos portal, and how the costs you will have to pay are distributed.

Sample Costs

When we talk about "samples" we don't mean what you're probably thinking: free samples. Instead we mean the need to have a small trial order, so as to "prove" the market for that particular product. We are sure that you will not want to run the risk of buying products for thousands of euros, only to find that nobody will be willing to buy them!

For this purpose, we recommend that you find your suppliers on the main industry portals, such as Alibaba, the largest network of suppliers in the world, mainly in Asia. Moreover, this is certainly not the only area where you can find useful suppliers for your purpose: think of trade fairs or the possibility of searching Google and specialized sites, with specific services for this need (some free, some for a fee).

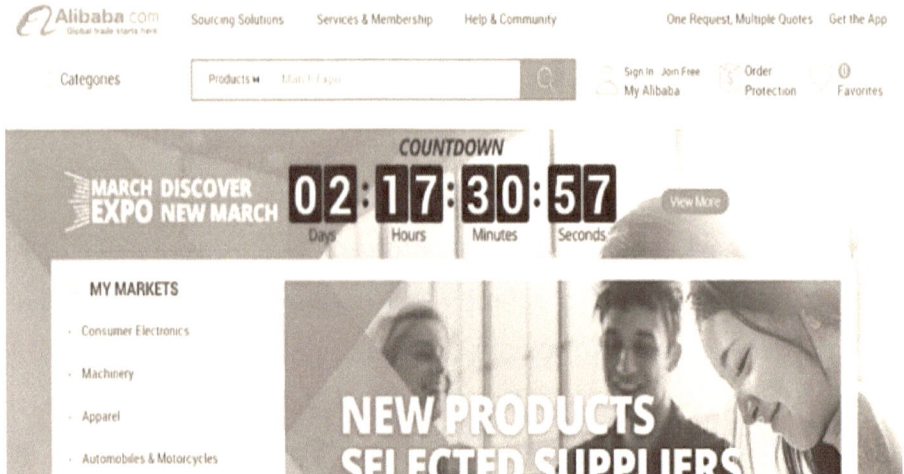

Once you have identified your supplier to "test", place small orders to evaluate the quality of the goods you are deciding to import. Then try to place orders from multiple suppliers, choosing your favorite based on the price and communication skills that your partner will be able to express: a supplier who strives to be clear in the conditions (not only in the economic ones) and it is particularly timely, it is a real ally for your commercial success.

Evaluate the prices of the products, whether there are discounts for larger orders and what the shipping conditions are. So ask for a timely quote and, when you are sufficiently convinced that you have all the information you need for an appropriate analysis of your supplier, proceed with the order and sell the products, in order to understand whether or not there is a real demand for that kind of merchandise.

Of course, at this stage it is not possible to estimate a reliable cost, given that a lot could depend on what you have in mind to develop as a characteristic business. Let's assume, however, that you want to make at least 200 dollars.

Amazon seller account costs

Among the main costs to be incurred to sell on Amazon there is of course the one linked to the price of your seller plan. The Basic Account has no fixed costs but provides a fixed closing commission per item sold equal to 0.99 euros. The Pro account, on the other hand, has a monthly subscription fee of € 39 + VAT, but no fixed closing fee per item sold.

Imagine we want to open a Pro account, so we budget 39 euros as account costs.

Be careful, though: this is not the only commission you will have to pay in the event of a sale! taking care, however, at least for the moment, of the start-up phase alone, we neglect these burdens.

Costs of EAN and UPC codes

If you want to sell your product on Amazon, it must have a GTIN code (UPC, ISBN or EAN). This is an essential requirement for which Amazon will obligatorily require you to fulfill, and which could therefore expose you to a small additional commission. In particular, in order to avoid confusion between the various codes, we remind you that UPC is the universal product code, ISBN is the international standard number of the book (it is therefore used only for publishing products) and EAN is the European number of article (EAN).

Now, considering that Amazon uses these codes and numbers to identify the exact item you want to sell, you can only equip yourself with this code. But at what price?

By registering and associating with GS1, which is the global point of reference for the attribution of the codes in question, you will pay a starting membership fee of € 395 (the fee is proportionate to your company's turnover), and € 95 in subsequent years. In return you will get access to 1,000 EAN codes. If, however, you have lower needs, you can use other sites that sell the codes at a single price between 2 and 10 euros, depending on the quantity purchased. Let's assume that you want to sell only two types of products, resulting in a budget of 20 euros.

In some cases you can even sell your products without an EAN code. You can learn more about the Amazon Brands Registry page.

Photography costs

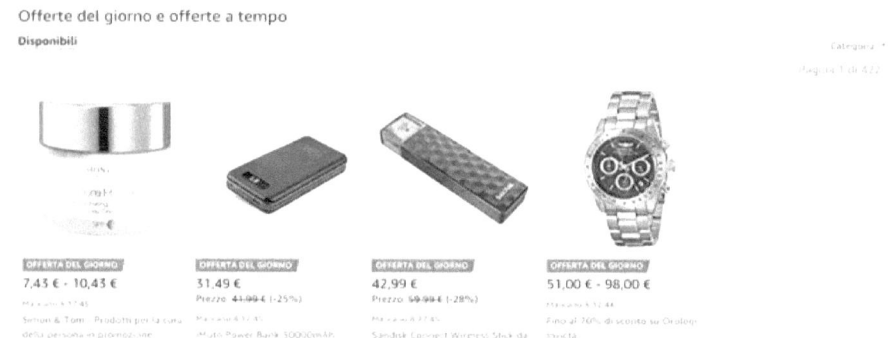

When you sell on Amazon, you're competing against other sellers who sell similar products to yours. It is therefore essential to be able to stand out. But how?

One of the simplest and most appealing methods is to present your products with useful photos to "attract" your customer and invite them to watch your ad. To do this, you can of course pay a professional to take pictures of your products but ... he would probably have an excessive rate in relation to your initial budget.

An intermediate solution between a professional photograph and a "do-it-yourself" photograph, which could really give you results of great satisfaction, is to use online photo services like the excellent one of Virtual Graphics. This is a high quality photo shoot that will take care of designing for you the best graphic content for your sale on Amazon: all you have to do is buy the quantity of photos you want, send some information that you will need to share with photographers and send the product you want to sell.

The cost of this service is as follows:
Of course, there are also alternative services, even in Italy, that will prevent you from sending products abroad. However, their cost is always around 15 euros per photo, with a minimum of 3 photos. Assuming a budget of 100 dollars that will also allow us to have explanatory photos and other optimized graphic contents.

Logo and branding costs

Another cost item that we advise you to include in your budget is linked to the logo and brand design of your product.

We advise you to do so by contacting a good designer, who will be able to structure the logo for you in a relatively short time, and maybe in the future it will still be useful for infographics, other content, and so on. Finding a good freelance for this goal is quite simple, considering the high number of specialized portals and forums dedicated to this purpose. Indicating how much a new logo will cost you is rather difficult, but on these services the starting cost is 30-50 euros.

In light of the above, we can therefore state that in order to profitably and regularly start a business on Amazon, you should allocate an initial budget of 450 - 500 euros. Besides, unfortunately, the costs related to the management of your VAT number.

VAT number costs

We have deliberately left this theme for last, as it is certainly the one most able to impact on the profitability of your online business. However, this is not a cost exclusively linked to Amazon: if it is true that to sell on Amazon you need a VAT position, it is also true that the same position will be useful for every sales activity and that, therefore, in many cases it would be wrong bring these

charges so directly to the marketplace.

However, given that we are trying to give you a fairly complete overview of everything you have to deal with to sell on Amazon, we can only share some thoughts with you. First, opening the

Ivadi game by itself does not imply sustaining the initial costs. The model can be downloaded from the Revenue Agency website, fill in and submit to the territorially competent body for tax

domicile.

However, from that moment on you will probably need the services of an accountant who can handle all tax and social security obligations for you. The cost may vary depending on the service you choose to identify: in principle, the fee for the professional

starts at 80/100 euros per month.

In addition to the cost of opening the VAT number and the fees of the accountant, there is also the minimal INPS

fixed of about $ 3700 per year for all merchants.

DO I NEED A VAT CARD
TO SELL ON AMAZON?

At this point, someone might wonder if it is necessary to have the VAT number to sell on Amazon, perhaps calling into question the "known" threshold of € 5,000 a year in revenue as a discriminating factor for opening or not the position with the Revenue.

Well, the time has come to make definitive clarity: if you want to be in good standing with the Tax and sell on Amazon you will necessarily have to open VAT number. In fact, in this hypothesis you will not be able to use the occasional services with withholding tax, so that the famous limit of 5,000 euros which exempts from the opening of the VAT number in this case cannot be used.

The sale of a product on Amazon is in fact a purely commercial activity and, consequently, you will have to comply with all the formalities required by the current tax system. It follows that in addition to the VAT number, you will need to present the start of activity report, register with the Business Register and regularize your position at INPS (on which you will have to pay the related contributions).

PRODUCT SEARCH

At this point, let's try to understand how to get the best from your online sales activities on Amazon by starting to focus on finding the product to place on the marketplace (unless you already have pretty clear ideas about this). In this sense, know that the commercial hypotheses to be developed can arrive at any time and from any place. Let us learn more!

WHERE TO FIND PRODUCT IDEAS

As we mentioned a few lines ago, the new ideas for a product to sell on Amazon can come to 360 degrees! For example, they can do it when you are at a friend's house, when you are out shopping, when you are surfing the Internet or when you are watching TV.

The best thing we advise you to do is create a long list of product ideas (at least 20) and then narrow the field starting from this fence. The approach that we suggest you then carry out is to find products that are already guaranteeing good sales levels and that have verifiable commercial data. Of course, the same products will have to be potentially modifiable, perhaps with a slight substantial change, and the addition of your logo and your brand.

It is not advisable to instead go in search of products that "you believe" can sell well or that "you would like" to sell: starting a business is a difficult task, and it is better not to make an important decision on the basis of "hope" alone. Better to think about numbers and statistics. But how?

PRODUCT ANALYSIS AND KEYWORDS

Imagining that you have already extracted the list of 20 product ideas that we suggested above, we proceed with the analysis of the keywords by doing a search for your first product. The objective must be to understand how much that product is sold and, above all, at what price and how many reviews it has obtained: a mix of determinants that will provide you with very valid information on the vitality of the segment and the depth of the market. In the hope, perhaps, that of the first 10 results that will appear under the keyword "obtained" from the product you want to sell, no more than 8 have less than 100 reviews. But why is analyzing reviews so important?

COMPETITION ANALYSIS

Evaluating the strength of the competition based on the number of reviews that a competitor product has already acquired is important because it is precisely on the reviews that customers make their purchasing decisions. Now, consider that getting a lot of reviews will take you a lot of time to "accumulate", and therefore going "against" a competition that can boast hundreds of reviews could prove a difficult battle to conduct.

Therefore analyze your competition carefully. In addition to the first results that the marketplace will be able to share with you, enter the sales category that interests you and try to understand who are the producers of the "bestsellers" of the one you are going to populate.

MARKETS ANALYSIS AND JUNGLESCOUT SALES ESTIMATE

At this point we want to recommend you a very interesting free service, which will allow you to analyze how large the market is, and how much your competitors are selling. The service we are talking about is the, that thanks to an easy use and a discreet reliability, will give you a general indication regarding how many sales are the sellers that are in a determined position in "ranking" on the single categories of Amazon. But what does it mean? And how to use this feature?

Notwithstanding that from the Junglescout sales estimates you don't have to wait for the precise data to the unit, the service is really useful to be able to understand how "alive" the market is for a given product category.

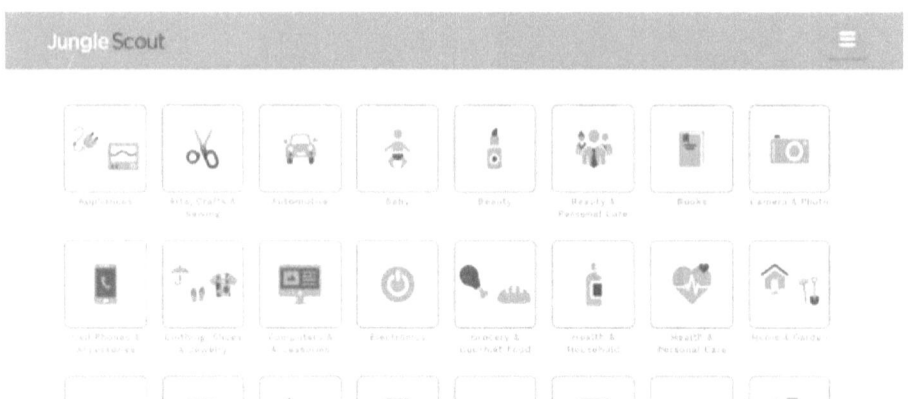

It is very simple to use them: once you have identified the product you would like to sell on Amazon, carried out an analysis of the keywords and competitors, log in to Junglescout and select the "parent" category of your product. At that point, you will have to enter in the field "Enter sales rank" the position number in the ranking of the competing product whose sales you want to estimate: you can find it in the product detail page, where the ranking in the sales ranking will appear internal of the category.

Indicate that number in the form and click on "Find out now!". Junglescout will provide you with an estimate of the monthly sales of that particular product: a figure that you can use to realize how large that market is!

Once this is done, repeat the same operation for the first 10 competitors on that specific product. Your goal should be to discover hundreds of sales a month on various products: for example, it might be helpful and comforting to know that there are at least 1,200 sales per month on that product, or 40 sales per day. Not bad, right? If the numbers fall far below this statistic, it means that sales tend to get rather low and that there is not much demand for that product.

Another aspect that you should check is the depth of the market, that is, the good spread of these sales. If in fact there are 1,200 sales in all, but the first two products on the list absorb 1,000 of those sales, it means that sales are not very well distributed and that, in summary, unless you are in the first or second position, you will not have much hope of placing your products on the market. So what we want to see from this analysis is that sales are fairly well distributed among the top 5 places.

PRODUCT SEASONALITY ANALYSIS

The next consideration in your product search should be the seasonality of the goods. Think about the lights of Christmas trees: sales figures for November and December will be extraordinary, because maybe you will have statistics of 6,000 units a month, or more. With the illusion that this is a huge great opportunity. However, you will also notice that in January the situation will be reversed: sales will almost disappear.

Therefore, our advice is to identify whether a product is seasonal or not and if, therefore, it only sells during certain periods of the year or if it sells everything during the year. A great tool to learn more is to use Google Trend: type in the product you want to examine and take a look at the chart, which shows the search volume for that particular asset. Of course, with this we do not want to advise you to stay away from seasonal products, but only to focus strategic attention on what you will have to do accordingly!

If you've come this far, you'll probably have realized that the hardest thing about starting an Amazon business is, ... starting an Amazon business! However, don't give up: this preliminary phase may seem difficult and unsatisfactory, but the more you can verify sales now, the easier your task will be in the following steps.

Drawing conclusions, use our previous suggestions

to find products that:

• You can sell at a price between 20 and 200 euros;

• They are light, small and easy to sell;

• Have estimated sales of at least 10 units per day;

• They can guarantee you a margin of at least 30%, with sales prices at least equal to 3 times the price you purchase;

• They can be shipped by air;

• They have less than 100 reviews.

SUPPLIER SEARCH

Now that you have a product in mind, it's time to find a supplier that works for you. Fortunately, there are some places where you can find many (though not all of the expected quality): think of Alibaba, Aliexpress, Globalsources, or even trade shows and the many services you can find on Google. Let us learn more!

WHERE TO FIND SUPPLIERS

As we were able to introduce, finding suppliers is easy, finding good suppliers is a little less. For example, Alibaba is by far the largest place where you can draw on potential business contacts: just type in the product you are looking for and, in a few moments, a world of incredible varieties will open up before you. However, not all suppliers on Alibaba have the same quality level. So how do you find a good supplier that fits your needs?

The rules for finding a good supplier on Alibaba are more or less the same cautions that you should take into consideration if you want to find a good supplier on Globalsources or other services. For exhibition convenience, let's focus on Alibaba anyway, given that you will have no trouble declines with regard to eBay and other e-commerce portals.

So try to find a good supplier by selecting those that:

• **have positive feedback: fame is important. It aims only at suppliers who have at least 95% positive feedback, and who has thousands of evaluations. Another element that we advise you to keep in mind when evaluating a supplier is the number of years of activity: better focus on sellers who have more history, more evaluations and a high rate of feedback. Moreover, Alibaba will allow you to order sellers based on the evaluation (seller rat-**

ing) saving you a lot of time;

• sell at the "right" price: buying from a supplier that offers its products at an "too" low price to be true is not an appropriate behavior. Move with great caution, as sometimes - especially if it has been on the market for a short time - a supplier who sells at very low prices is a supplier who wants to leave his mark or who sells extremely low quality products. Therefore compare the prices on different sellers: if the supplier you are considering has a sale price of its products much lower than the average, it is probably placing non-original or lower quality products. For example, AliExpress offers a tool that filters products based on prices: just go to the "price" field on the product page and see how many people bought that product in that price range. If few people have done it for that low price range ... maybe it's not a good deal;

• respond to your contact requests: a correct communication with the supplier is one of the fundamental elements of attention when you are choosing your strategic partners. Write to the supplier, ask him also very specific details on shipping, delivery and product quality and evaluate the responsiveness and quality of the response.

Obviously, these are not the only aspects you should consider in order to find a good supplier. It is however a small group of priority elements that you should not lose sight of. And, moreover, these are not the only steps you could take to find quality suppliers: on the Italian or European market, for example, you can find suppliers able to become your new partners practically anywhere, such as in fairs or artisan exhibitions, in export events and in all those meeting occasions that we recommend you start attending.

HOW TO NEGOTIATE WITH THE SUPPLIER

Following the instructions we have shared with you above, we suggest that you contact 5 different suppliers. To each of them, you can ask different questions such as:

• do you offer a sample?

• How much does a sample sent to this postal code cost?

• what price do you pay me for 500 units of product?

• what price do you pay me for 1,000 units of product?

• Can I make a first order of only 10 units of product? At what price?

In addition, you can also ask for something more specific, such as product customization policies (we'll talk about the private label in the next section), and everything that comes to mind. In this sense, we advise you to ask all these questions together, in a single email, so as not to go back and forth with communications. So consider their answer: do they communicate adequately and clearly? Have they answered all your questions or just given you a generic answer?

Try to negotiate sample prices, suggesting that you are comparing more offers. Always try to check off the best price, and get a sample as soon as possible, as you will first get a sample and you can go ahead with the next steps first. When you are satisfied with the sample and the supplier, proceed with the report stating that you would like to place your first order. Also in this second phase you will be able to negotiate the price.

Another element that we advise you to evaluate with your possible partner is the negotiation of payment terms. Often you can come to an agreement with an advance payment of 30%, and then 70% before shipping the product. Sometimes you can check off only 50% up-front and 50% on delivery. In terms of payment methods, PayPal is certainly good for the sample phase, but for larger orders, also due to its high commissions, it is better to focus on bank transfers which have fixed amounts and not in percentage terms.

Making a private label

A good alternative - moreover, more and more
accessible - that you could try, is to create private

label products. But what is meant by that?

In summary (we will explore this in a separate guide) private label products are branded items that a supplier can produce on behalf of others. In other words, by descending into the context in which you are probably moving, you can have your logo and your distinctive marks imprinted on the design of an existing product, which the supplier will develop for you. The advantages are considerable: you will be able to obtain a "private brand" without committing yourself to a product development process

which, in other cases, would have required more time and money.

Even at this juncture, China (which we have already mentioned in relation to Alibaba) could be an ideal place to find a supplier able to apply private labels to factory-designed products that are already readily available.

Therefore, be careful to repeat the steps above in order to find the most convenient private label suppliers, and pause with them, analyzing the type of printing, colors, positioning of distinctive signs, graphics, and so on. Then send a sample to evaluate the quality.

ACCOUNT OPENING ON AMAZON

At this point, you are ready to enter the operational phase: open an Amazon account and configure all the main aspects of managing your presence on the marketplace.

Let's see together what the different types of accounts are, how to open a new merchant account on Amazon and how to focus on the dashboard.

Different types of accounts

Currently Amazon has two different types of merchant accounts, Base and Pro, able to adapt to the specific needs of each seller. By inviting you to learn more about the terms and conditions of service on the page linked above, we summarize here:

• Account Base: it is the ideal account for those who sell small quantities (less than 40 sales per month). Its main benefit is that you will not have to pay any fees until you sell something. For each sale there is in fact a fixed closing commission per item sold equal to 0.99 euros.

• Account Pro: it is the ideal account for those who sell large quantities (more than 40 sales per month). There is no fixed closing fee per item sold but, on the other hand, there is a monthly subscription fee of 39 € on Amazon. In addition, compared to the Basic account, the Pro account will allow you to sell products in all Amazon categories, obtain eligibility for 1-Click purchases, have access to order reports and any feeds connected to them, upload your inventory and offers through automated tools (large file uploads), have access to Seller Central API and Amazon's Web Services.

	Account di Base Vendi piccole quantità	Account Pro Vendi grandi quantità
Adatto a venditori che indentono effettuare	meno di 40 vendite al mese	più di 40 vendite al mese
Vantaggi	Non dovrai pagare fino a quando non venderai qualcosa	L'offerta più conveniente per grandi volumi di affari
RIEPILOGO TARIFFE ¹ le tariffe dipendono dalle categorie		
Quota di abbonamento mensile di Vendita su Amazon		39,00 EUR
Commissione di chiusura fissa per articolo venduto	0,99 EUR	

In light of this, our suggestion is to aim for the opening of a Pro account, which will allow you to access more complete tools and, above all, not having to undergo pricing for sold units that would make your business less convenient in case - we hope it's yours! - high sales. If instead you are hesitant about sales volumes, in the early stages you will be able to choose a Basic Account, which you can then convert into a Pro at a later time.

How to open an account

All you have to do to register on Amazon is to connect to the Amazon Services page. You'll have a screen like this in front of you:

At this point click on Register Now and, if you want, first check "I want to sell on 5 European sites" (by contrast, don't put any check if you want to sell only on Amazon). The difference is that if you check this box you can sell your products on all five of Amazon's European marketplaces (Amazon.co.uk, Amazon.de, Amazon.fr, Amazon.it and Amazon.es) and reach more potentials. buyers.

In short, by checking this box you can actually have the opportunity to sell on all these marketplaces without paying any additional subscription fees. Moreover, even in the management phase there will be no particular complications, given that you will only have to create offers on your main marketplace: those deemed suitable will be automatically recreated on the other four marketplaces using the "Create offers internationally" tool. Keep in mind, however, that you can enable your account for international sales even later.

Now that you've clicked on Register, you'll find yourself in front of this screen:

If you are already registered with Amazon (because you have already purchased from this service or have thought about doing it), you can create a Seller account using the same credentials. Otherwise, or if you want to keep your personal account separate from the "corporate" one, you can proceed by clicking "Create your Amazon account". A brief phase of completing the registration will follow with all your personal and professional data (keep them at hand) and the verification of credentials. The data that will be asked of you is:

·Credit card;

·Telephone number;

· Company information;

· Information on the contact person;

· Information on the beneficial owner;

·Banking data.Fatto ciò, sei pronto per vendere su Amazon!

PRODUCT SHIPMENT

One of the most important aspects that you will have to try to clarify before selling your products is related to the management of logistics and shipments. In this regard, Amazon offers you two distinct processes (FBA and FBM), each of which characterized by elements of advantage and attention.
We try to understand in more detail what it is, and how you can relate positively with them!

Types of shipping

A few lines ago we introduced two distinct shipping solutions from Amazon, FBA and FBM. The abbreviation FBA, Fulfillment by Amazon, will allow you to manage the process entirely at the marketplace, which will therefore take care of managing the inventory, warehouse, shipments and customer service.

In short, by using the FBA service you will need to ship your products to Amazon's distribution center, which will store them until there is an order to be sent. Once the order is received, the product will be packaged and shipped directly from Amazon.
On the other hand, FBM, Fulfillment by Merchant, means that the whole process must be managed by the seller. Therefore, you will have to take care of inventory, storage and shipping in person. As you can guess, each alternative process will not be without reflections: let's see them together.

FBA - Fulfillment by Amazon: Amazon Logistics

The FBA service is developed through a series of consecutive easy-to-understand steps. First of all, you will have to send your products directly to the storage center indicated here. Amazon will have control of the inventory, being able to monitor what the movements are carried out day after day. When the customer orders your product, Amazon will therefore take charge of the appearance of the preparation, packaging and shipping of the goods. Amazon will also take care of customer service and return management.

As can be guessed, one of the main benefits of being an FBA vendor is linked to the possibility of delegating to Amazon all the tasks related to warehouse management, shipments and returns. Furthermore, being an FBA vendor allows its products to become eligible for Prime, increasing the possibility of contacting potential buyers. Also of importance is the benefit linked to post-sales management, which often represents a particular annuity for sellers.

Of course, among the "disadvantages" of this sales and shipping management method is the fact that you will need to ship your products to the Amazon Fulfillment Center, and pay a monthly / annual fee to the marketplace (which you can estimate using the calculator of the rates you find here). In our opinion, however, this is a small burden that could be amply rewarded: the statistics tell us that FBA sellers have higher conversion rates, and that they can devote more time to other activities, considering that all responsibility for the above actions will fall entirely on Amazon.

FBM – Fulfillment by Merchant

The alternative to FBA is the FBM service - Fulfillment by Merchant. That is, the process of managing the sale and shipment entirely by the seller.

This is a choice that many sellers prefer to embrace, thus increasing the degree of control over each stage of the product placement process on the market, avoiding having to send their goods to Amazon's center and avoiding the expense of the service FBA. Furthermore, being an FBM seller does not preclude entry into the Prime category, although it will be much more difficult than those with FBA status.

On the other hand, the very need to fully manage every aspect of the sale could be the main disadvantage. The seller will have to deal with every item, perhaps trying to avoid shipping delays, offering immediate responses to orders and providing positive feedback.

How to ship products to Amazon according to their terms

Using the FBA service is quite simple. First, you need to register with an Amazon merchant account, and then request activation of the Amazon Logistics service during the same registration process, or at a later time. By doing this, you will have to accept the terms and conditions of service that - among other things - prevent some goods from being able to use the FBA service: to take a look at the complete list and all the details on the requirements

and restrictions of Amazon Logistics, we advise you to click here.

Once that is done, in the offers tabs, in the Shipping Mode section, you will have to tick the option "In case of sale, I want Amazon to manage the shipment and provide customer support". If you are using one of the inventory file templates to present your products, you will need to enter "AMAZON_EU" in the "Logistic center ID" field in order to include these products in Amazon's Logistics offers.

If you want to take a complete look at the Logistics service terms, with a rich list of FAQs that will take away

all your doubts, try looking at this page.

OPTIMIZED PRODUCT PAGE CREATION ON AMAZON

Before giving you some suggestions on how to improve your first sales management steps on Amazon, we want to share some thoughts on the correct realization of a product page on the marketplace. Let's start with an overview of its general features!

Brand name

The name of the brand is an extremely important aspect in proposing a product for sale. But how to choose one that can go really well for your trade policies? Below, we have reported for you 5 characteristics that we believe a good name should have:

• Acknowledgment: choose a unique name, which is not similar or comparable to other pre-existing names, especially if they are part of your sector.

• Communication: identifies an evocative, descriptive name that can convey emotions to your potential customer.

• Simplicity: the name should be easy to remember. A feature that, ultimately, very often coincides with the criterion of brevity.

• Lack of ambiguity: the name should be unambiguous, both phonetic and meaningful.
• Online usability: the ideal would be for your brand to correspond to a .it domain (if you want to sell only in Italy) or .com (if you want to sell all over the world) free, in order to develop or continue running a site web owner.

Product   title

As you can easily imagine, the title of your product should clearly indicate what you are trying to sell or, better what your potential customers are looking for and how you can satisfy their needs and in which aspects you are better than your competitors (eg. does not smell, washable, …). The title must be brief but sufficiently comprehensive, as well as able to bring the brand back. Overall, try to limit the title to no more than 20 words.

PHOTOGRAPHS PRODUCED

Although it is a priority element, unfortunately there are still many vendors who "forget" (or underestimate) the essentiality of the visual presentation of products. Not only will it be possible to show off high-resolution photos of the products, and be able to concentrate on various aesthetic and substantial aspects of the goods, it will allow your potential customer to realize what he has in front of you, but you will also allow to reduce the gap between expectations and ... when the customer will receive the goods at home.

Therefore, we invite you to be scrupulous in enriching your product page with several high quality photos, taking your product from different angles and maybe showing different useful elements, which customers reasonably expect to find in the product sheet (think, for example, at the back of the packages).

If then you have doubts about your photographic effectiveness, as we have already had occasion to remind you a few lines ago, it is better to opt for an expert and professional service: it will be worth it, compared to a small initial effort to be included in the budget!

PRODUCT DESCRIPTION

The description of the product is - as you can easily guess - one of the most important elements in providing more value added to your sale. It is probable that, in drafting the description of your property, you may be seized by doubts and anxieties, and perhaps by the desire to indicate every minimum technical detail, with the risk of being "too" exhaustive and, therefore, providing super-fluous information.

But how to find the right way? Doing it is quite simple: our suggestion is to summarize a product description marrying one that is not too long, but which contains all the features that your customer expects to read.

Therefore, try to identify yourself in the role of the buyer, and identify the elements you would like to find in the merchandise for sale. Then take care of the display, avoiding to structure the description in a single block of text: use paragraphs and short sentences, highlight some more relevant concepts in bold, create bulleted lists, and so on.
Finally, in the final part of the description, invite the customer to buy now to get an exclusive and momentary offer that you have created for him.

SHIP

Your customer has a characteristic: he wants to receive his purchased product as soon as possible, in the way he prefers. Precisely for this reason, take care to give your customers the greatest choice in receiving the goods. If, in particular, you are dealing with shipping and logistics with an FBM approach, take care - preventively - to make agreements with couriers able to keep the promises you will have to make towards users.

BEING FIRST IN AMAZON: STRATEGIES AND OPTIMIZATIONS

When you start managing your business on Amazon, there are two things you will desperately need: sales and reviews. Both obtained on desirable thresholds, you will in fact have achieved the necessary momentum to position yourself well on the most popular search terms, be found by more customers and, therefore, make sales.

Now, to learn more, you should take into account that the way customers find products on Amazon is, in the majority, that of typing in the search bar the product they are looking for, selecting a product from the list and, then , consider whether to buy that good or not. By supporting this, your goal can only be to make sure that your ad appears in the top positions when your potential customer types in the product name.

If, for example, your product is a pair of leather gloves for men, you should probably do everything to position yourself with the keyword "men's leather gloves". This way, when a customer types this search term on Amazon, he can see your ad among the best results. Considering that your potential customer might do slightly different research, you will also have to try to position yourself on different keywords, such as - to take our example again - "adult leather gloves", and so on.

But why is it so important to try to position yourself "correctly"? You can probably arrive at this evaluation by putting yourself in the shoes of a customer: would you ever see the listings on page 20 or 50? Probably not. And, amplifying the theme, it is not

wrong to say that those ads will never be seen by customers.

Now, the only valid way to start climbing the charts and appear on the first page, where you will have most of the commercial feedback, is to get sales. And that's why sales are one of the most important things to get at the beginning of your adventure on Amazon: once you have this visibility, you will also get more customers, and with more customers, you will also gain more sales

force.

But how can you support the launch of your product with the

right strategies and optimizations? Let us learn more!

PRODUCT LAUNCH
AND PROMOTION

Before leaving you with some final reflection, we wanted to share with you 6 practical approaches that will accompany the launch of your product more effectively. These are rules that will probably improve your sales and your popularity on Amazon, and that we advise you to follow if you want to be fully able to lead the start of your business project with the right firm hand.
Are you ready?

ACQUIRE REVIEWS

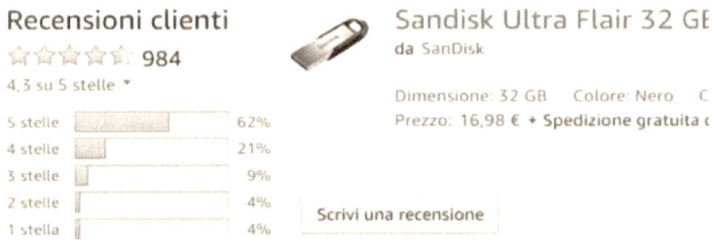

We have already mentioned how on Amazon customers buy from products that have a high number of positive reviews. And that's why it's really important for you to get sales and reviews in good quantity. But (of the sales we will deal with in the next paragraph) how can you get good reviews on Amazon?

The evidence is that succeeding is increasingly difficult. And certainly not because the products you want to sell are of poor quality. The "problem" - so to speak - is that customer expectations are on average always higher, and that when your customers have decided to buy your product, they probably have obtained very in-depth information about it. Which, of course, should lead you to sell a product that is able to reflect their wishes, by inserting (we talked about it a little while ago) in the product sheet any useful information to improve the level of transparency.

In this scenario, there is of course much you can do to induce the customer to leave a good review. And to get this result, try to start from a basic reflection: the customer wants not only a product in line with his own expectations, but an overall shopping experience that is satisfying, enriched by constant, reliable and correct relationships with the seller.

All this leads us to a very important suggestion: to improve the flow of communications with your client through transactional emails and "hope" that these will help you in obtaining a good result.

Transactional emails are communications that you will send based on a specific user action. Their importance is remarkable: they are traditionally the emails that record the highest opening rate, since they are emails that contain information of relevance to the user. Think, for example, of the communications your customer receives as confirmation of a purchase.

Now, considering that in most cases these are emails that the user expects, and from which the customer expects you to confirm that the purchase and delivery process is going smoothly, the non-receipt or receipt with incongruous content could leave him disappointed, lowering the degree of trust towards you.

Remember therefore to always send emails to the customers, avoiding perhaps to make the opposite mistake, or to send too many: we advise instead to limit the flow to a first email to confirm the purchase, a second email to confirm the shipment occurred , a third email with updates on the status of the shipment, a fourth email to request a review.
In particular, be careful not to neglect the emails that more than others can induce your customer to leave a review: those sent when you know that the user has received his order. It is in that moment, in fact, that the customer has the greatest possibility and desire to leave feedback and, therefore, you should exploit it by sending an email containing a kind review request on the experience had with your store / product.

SET PROMOTIONS

In the last paragraph we mentioned how important it is to focus your attention on the need to get as many sales and positive reviews in the first phase of your Amazon project. Store our short thoughts on reviews, we can only deal with the other big aspect of "pushing" your product, sales.

Well, one of the most suitable strategies to improve the sales levels of your product at an early stage of market placement is promotion. For example, you can offer your products with very strong discounts (up to 50%) on a limited number of units, in order to obtain those sales that you would otherwise have hardly been able to obtain. You can therefore offer coupons on sector websites, push discount codes on social networks, and so on.

You will soon notice that by offering these discounts, you will be able to guarantee a greater opportunity to carry out many sales, and in any case much more than you could get from leaving your product at full price.

The above also means that you will probably start losing margins on initial sales. Therefore, it is important to have an ad hoc budget: always remember that you need these initial sales to get your ad started on the right foot and rank it for some keywords so you can start getting natural organic sales.

Promotion with PPC Amazon

Another way to adequately push your product for sale is to evaluate specific promotional strategies with the Amazon advertising platform, with PPC (or pay-per-click) operation: your ad can be viewed above all others, in exchange for a burden that we advise you to budget.

The use of PPC campaigns in Amazon is simple, as the process is easy to configure. All you have to do is select the keywords with which you would like to be viewed in a "sponsored" manner and how much you are willing to pay to be shown under that keyword. In some ways (not all!) The mechanism is therefore similar to that of Google AdWords.

Now, there are two very simple initiatives that Amazon has prepared for you. Let us first understand what the automatic campaigns are, and after the automatic emails.

PPC automatic campaigns

If you are convinced that Amazon's PPC campaign can finally create a good advantage for your promotional strategy, all you have to do is enter the seller central, access the advertising campaign management section and then proceed with creating it. You will be able to give a name to your campaign, and a daily budget of how much you would like to spend. So, for example, you could indicate that starting today you are willing to spend 20 euros.

It is at this stage that you can indicate whether you want an automatic or manual campaign. Our suggestion, at least at the beginning, is to set up an automatic campaign: select this option and click Continue. Now you can select the product you want to "sponsor" and select a default offer. Let us assume, in our example, 1 euro.

At this point, be careful: the above does not mean that you are willing to pay 1 euro for each view. It just means that 1 euro is what you are willing to pay as a ceiling: therefore, if the person before you for that particular placement attempt offered 30 euro cents, your actual cost could be 31 cents. It is precisely for this reason that we advise you to act prudently: make offers that are not too high and see how your visualizations behave.

If after a few days you realize that you are not getting many impressions or views, the reason could be that your default offer is too low, and other people are making higher bids than you. Therefore, your ad is not shown to potential customers. With this information base, you can therefore try to raise your offer a little more.

By doing so, you will have the concrete possibility of reserving many benefits for you. First, automatic campaigns are really easy to set up and don't take much time. Secondly, they will also start working for you on the data collection front. At the beginning, in fact, you will not be aware of what are the keywords that people click most to find your ad. With an automatic campaign, Amazon will suggest you which keywords you think are the most relevant.
After running this campaign for at least a week, you can then download a report that will show all the keywords for which Amazon showed you. You can therefore take that information, select the keywords with the best performances and then insert them into your manual campaign, where you will have more con-

trol over how much you can spend on each keyword.

PRODUCT LAUNCH COSTS

At this stage of our in-depth analysis we can only emphasize how, at least at the beginning, your PPC campaigns and your promotional initiatives will cost you a little money. Sales are probably not going to be very profitable, but - remember - it is very important that you have an initial marketing budget, in order to positively push your ad.

The long-term effects that you will be able to achieve are well known: you will begin to rise to an ever higher level for many of the keywords that people use to find your product; once you start classifying yourself for many different keywords and you will start to have a good pool of reviews, you will also begin to receive sales on an organic, natural basis. In other words, once the first step has been successfully completed, you will get sales without spending (almost) nothing, but simply because people will start looking for your product on Amazon.

So, don't make a common mistake, which many entrepreneurs unfortunately repeat: some people, as you will notice, hesitate to make initial promotions or conduct PPC campaigns because they fear losing a bit of money. The result is that they remain blocked on page 20 or 30, where there is no visibility, and where they will not get sales. Then set a budget for the product launch: it will be worth it!

If you have read all the parts of this guide carefully, you should have understood how to find a new product idea, how to choose your next suppliers, how to handle shipping and logistics, how to set up a good product page and how to push initial sales. And then? Often, the work of managing your business on Amazon consists in adapting to the evolutionary context: it continues to follow these rules and ... to follow us: we will soon face every other aspect related to improving the opportunities for success of your online entrepreneurial initiative!

www.ingramcontent.com/pod-product-compliance
Lightning Source LLC
Chambersburg PA
CBHW021042180526
45163CB00005B/2246